MR MIDSHIPMAN
HORNBLOWER

A sailing ship of war in the 1790s is not a comfortable place to be. You sleep below decks, where it is hot, airless, and smelly. The ceilings are so low that you can't even stand up straight. You eat salt meat and hard bread. You can drown if your ship sinks, you can be taken prisoner, you can be killed in battle . . . It is a hard, tough life, and you are lucky if you survive.

Horatio Hornblower wants to do more than just survive. He is only seventeen, the youngest midshipman on the ship, and he has a lot to learn. At first he is so miserable that he wants to die, but he learns how to survive, and he learns fast. He learns to be brave, and also generous; he learns when to take a chance, when to fight, and when not to fight.

And he has plenty of chances for learning – sailing through storms and through fog, fighting battles with the French, and then the Spanish, surviving as a prisoner of war . . .

OXFORD BOOKWORMS LIBRARY
Thriller & Adventure

Mr Midshipman Hornblower

Stage 4 (1400 headwords)

Series Editor: Jennifer Bassett
Founder Editor: Tricia Hedge
Activities Editors: Jennifer Bassett and Christine Lindop

C. S. FORESTER

Mr Midshipman
Hornblower

Retold by
Rosemary Border

OXFORD UNIVERSITY PRESS
2000

Oxford University Press
Great Clarendon Street, Oxford OX2 6DP

Oxford New York
Athens Auckland Bangkok Bogotá Buenos Aires Calcutta Cape Town
Chennai Dar es Salaam Delhi Florence Hong Kong Istanbul Karachi
Kuala Lumpur Madrid Melbourne Mexico City Mumbai Nairobi
Paris São Paulo Shanghai Singapore Taipei Tokyo Toronto Warsaw
and associated companies in
Berlin Ibadan

OXFORD and OXFORD ENGLISH
are trade marks of Oxford University Press

ISBN 0 19 423041 4

Original edition © The Estate of C. S. Forester
First published by Michael Joseph Ltd 1950
This simplified edition © Oxford University Press 2000

Second impression 2000

First published in Oxford Bookworms 1991
This second edition published in the Oxford Bookworms Library 2000

Illustrated by Gay Galsworthy
Map by Martin Ursell

The reference for the cover illustration has been taken from the television film
Hornblower, starring Ioan Gruffudd, Robert Lindsay, Dorain Healy, Denis Lawson,
Cherie Lunghi, Ronald Pickup, Antony Sher, Estelle Skornik, Peter Vaughan.
Executive Producers: Vernon Lawrence, Delia Fine. Producer: Andrew Benson.
Line Producer: Peter Richardson. Director: Andrew Grieve.

Typeset by Hope Services (Abingdon) Ltd
Printed in Spain

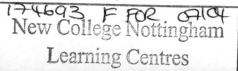

CONTENTS

1

The Even Chance

It was 1793, and England and France were deadly enemies. The French Revolution was now four years old, and a year ago the French people had cut off the head of their King. England, like other countries in Europe, was very much afraid of these violent and alarming changes. The idea of revolution was a dangerous disease, which other countries could catch. So England sent its men, its warships and its guns to fight the French on land and sea.

On this sunny January day in 1793, an English warship, the *Justinian*, was lying in Spithead harbour, near the city of Portsmouth. A small boat, rowed by two strong women, was moving towards the ship. The sea was usually calm in Spithead harbour, but today a wild wind was blowing, and the small boat danced madly on steep little waves. But the women knew their job, and slowly the boat came close to the big ship.

'Who's there?' came a call from the *Justinian*. The answering call from one of the women showed that the boat contained an officer.

Lieutenant Masters of the *Justinian* was old and grey. He had been fortunate to become a lieutenant, and he knew that he would never be a captain. However, this did not worry him, and he looked forward to meeting the new officer.

He saw a tall, thin young man with big feet, bony knees and elbows, and a white face, which had the greenish look of seasickness. Masters noticed, however, that the dark eyes in the white face were looking around with interest.

The young man climbed on board and came up to Masters. He touched his hat, opened his mouth and closed it again, too shy to speak.

'Your name?' said Masters.

'H–Horatio Hornblower, sir. Midshipman.'

'Welcome, Mr Hornblower.' Masters turned to the ship's boy. 'Boy! Show Mr Hornblower to the midshipmen's berth. Mr Hornblower, leave your bag there, and then come up and see me again.'

'Yes, sir,' answered the newcomer. Then he remembered he was speaking to an officer. Quickly correcting himself, he said, 'Aye, aye, sir,' and touched his hat again.

Hornblower followed the boy down several steep ladders to the midshipmen's berth on a lower deck. The ceiling was very low and Hornblower could not stand up straight. The only light came from two oil lamps on the ceiling. Six men were sitting round a table.

The boy disappeared and left Hornblower standing there. It was a moment before the man at the head of the table looked at him.

'Who are you?' he asked without much interest.

Hornblower felt his stomach turn over with seasickness. The midshipmen's berth was hot, airless and smelly, and although the ship was in the harbour, it was moving most uncomfortably.

'My name is Hornblower,' he said miserably.

At that moment a very large wave hit the ship. The deck moved uneasily under Hornblower's feet and he almost fell over.

'Well, well,' said a second man. 'Here's our latest midshipman. How old are you, boy?'

'S—seventeen, sir,' said Hornblower.

'Seventeen! You must start at twelve if you want to be a real seaman.'

'Yes, sir,' said Hornblower miserably. Then another terrible attack of seasickness hit him.

'Please excuse me—' he began. The others stared at him.

'My God!' shouted one of the midshipmen. 'He's seasick!'

'Seasick in Spithead harbour!' said another. 'What will he do when we *really* go to sea?'

And so Hornblower became famous as the midshipman who was seasick in Spithead. He was homesick too, and missed his family terribly. During the next few days, however, the seasickness disappeared and he slowly and painfully found his way around the ship. But he remained terribly lonely and friendless. The other midshipmen were much older than he was. Also, the *Justinian* was not a happy ship. Captain Keene was a sick man and spent a lot of his time in his cabin.

*And so Hornblower became famous as the midshipman who was
seasick in Spithead.*

'Well, Mr Hornblower,' said Captain Keene when at last he called the new officer to his cabin a few days later. 'You're seventeen, aren't you?'

'Yes, sir.'

'What did you like best at school?'

'Latin, sir.'

'Oh dear! Mathematics would be more useful to you.'

In his short time on the *Justinian* Hornblower had learnt to keep his mouth shut. He was in fact very good at mathematics, but he decided to let his captain find this out for himself.

'Well, obey orders, do your best and no harm will come to you. Goodbye, young man, and good luck.'

'No harm will come to you,' the captain had said; but he was wrong. The next day Mr Midshipman Simpson arrived, and Hornblower's life became very miserable indeed.

Simpson was the *Justinian's* oldest midshipman. He was a big, strong man of thirty-five, who had been sent to do the work of a lieutenant on another ship. The other midshipmen were very surprised when Simpson returned to the *Justinian* and took his seat at the head of the table. He had failed his examination to become a lieutenant and was now a midshipman again. He was naturally disappointed. He made all the midshipmen's lives miserable – and especially Hornblower's.

Simpson was not a clever man, but he knew how to find out people's secret fears and weaknesses – and then he could be both cruel and violent. Hornblower had thought he was unhappy before. After Simpson's arrival, however, he honestly wanted to die. The captain was too sick to notice, and his lieutenants were too lazy to do anything about it. Hornblower could not fight Simpson. Several other midshipmen had tried that without success. Each time Simpson was uninjured, while Lieutenant Masters noticed the loser's bruises and punished *him* instead of Simpson. All the other midshipmen burned with anger at the unfairness of it all.

Although the ship was in the harbour and not far from land, Hornblower could not escape. Running away was punishable by death, and although Hornblower wished for death he did not want his family to be ashamed of him. Friendless and miserable, he lay awake at night and wondered how he could kill himself.

One day, however, he and Simpson found themselves on land together. The two midshipmen had been sent, together with officers from other ships in the harbour, to collect new seamen for the warships.

'I feel at peace with the world,' said Simpson.

This was an unusual thing for him to say, but he was unusually comfortable. He was sitting in a pub in front of a welcoming fire, with a glass of hot whisky in front of him and his feet up on a chair. Hornblower, on the other side of the fireplace, drank his beer and watched Simpson. He realized with surprise that for the first time in several weeks his unhappiness was not quite so desperate. It was just a feeling of dull misery, like toothache.

The door opened and two officers from another ship came in. It was Lieutenant Chalk of the *Goliath* and one of his midshipmen, a man named Caldwell. Simpson introduced Hornblower to them.

'Mr Hornblower is famous,' Simpson added with a laugh, 'as the midshipman who was seasick in Spithead.'

'It could happen to anyone,' said Chalk politely. He sat down by the fire. 'It will be some time before our seamen arrive. So, would anyone like a game of cards? How about whist? I know Caldwell plays. What about you two?'

'It will pass the time,' said Simpson.

'Yes, please, sir,' said Hornblower warmly. His father had taught him to play whist. He was good at it and played whenever he had the chance.

They played for money, and soon Simpson was losing badly. Whist is not a game of chance, and stupid players do not usually win. Simpson, however, blamed everything on bad luck and ordered another large whisky.

Hornblower and Chalk were playing together against Simpson and Caldwell, and they were winning easily. Hornblower was lost in the enjoyment of his favourite game. Simpson, however, was both a bad drinker and a bad loser. He was becoming angrier and angrier, while his face turned from red to purple. At last he threw down his cards.

'It's no use playing with you, Hornblower!' he shouted. 'You know too much about this game. You know the backs of the cards as well as the fronts!'

There was an uncomfortable silence. Accusing somebody of cheating, Hornblower realized, was a matter of life or death – if he chose. Wild thoughts raced through his mind. He remembered his desperately unhappy life on the *Justinian*. He had often thought about death – and he had often wished that Simpson would die. Now, quite suddenly, he saw a way out of his miserable situation. He spoke quietly and clearly.

'Mr Chalk, Mr Caldwell, you heard that. Mr Simpson has just accused me of cheating at cards. There is only one answer to that.'

The others knew what he meant. There would have to be a duel between the two men. Chalk was worried.

'Come, come, Mr Hornblower,' he said smoothly. 'Mr Simpson didn't mean to accuse you of cheating. I'm sure he will explain.'

'Yes,' said Caldwell. 'Mr Simpson has had too much to drink. I'm sure you will excuse him. Let's order another bottle and drink it together as friends.'

'Of course,' said Hornblower carefully, 'if Mr Simpson will apologize at once.' He looked hard at Simpson and hoped that the older man would not apologize. Simpson did not. Instead he began to shout.

'Apologize to *you*, you miserable little nobody? I'd rather die!'

'You know the backs of the cards as well as the fronts!'
Simpson shouted at Hornblower.

'You heard that,' said Hornblower to the other officers. 'Mr Simpson refused to apologize. There will have to be a duel now.'

It was two days before the new seamen arrived, and during this time on land, Hornblower and Simpson lived the strange, unnatural life of two enemies before a duel. Hornblower carefully obeyed every order Simpson gave him, and Simpson gave his orders in an uncomfortable, self-conscious way. And during those two days Hornblower thought very coldly and carefully about this duel. He decided that he could not possibly lose. Here was the quick, easy death he had dreamed about – and the possibility of killing his enemy too. As soon as he returned to the *Justinian*, he appointed two other midshipmen as the seconds that every duellist had to have to assist him. Their names were Danvers and Preston and they hated Simpson too.

'Have you chosen your weapon yet?' asked Preston.

'Pistols,' said Hornblower.

'Can you shoot straight?' asked Danvers doubtfully. 'I'm sure Simpson can.'

'I've never tried,' said Hornblower. Then, as the others shook their heads, he added, 'I've thought of a way of giving each of us an even chance. Have two pistols, one loaded and the other unloaded. We choose our weapons without knowing which pistol is loaded. Then we stand one metre away from each other, and fire.'

'My God!' said Danvers.

'But one of you would be killed, for certain,' said Preston.

'Killing is what a duel is all about,' said Hornblower coldly. 'Go and ask Simpson's seconds and see if they agree.'

In less than an hour the conditions of the duel were known all over the ship. Perhaps it was to Simpson's disadvantage that he had no real friends in the midshipmen's berth. Certainly his seconds, Hether and Cleveland, agreed quite quickly to Hornblower's conditions. Lieutenant Masters, however, sent for Hornblower.

'The captain has ordered me to do my best to prevent this duel, Mr Hornblower,' he said carefully.

'Yes, sir.'

'Why are you doing this? I understand there were a few angry words over a game of cards.'

'Mr Simpson accused me of cheating, sir, in front of officers from another ship.'

'But must you fight a duel, Hornblower? Can't you just shake hands and forget all about it?'

'Of course, sir – if Mr Simpson will apologize.' As he said it, he knew he was safe. Simpson would rather die than apologize to Hornblower. Masters knew that too. He shook his head sadly.

'I see. So you won't change your mind?'

'No, sir.'

'Well, then, the captain has ordered me to be present at the duel. Please tell your seconds to arrange it for tomorrow morning.'

He looked very hard at Hornblower, searching for signs of weakness or fear. Hornblower showed none. He had an even chance of dying or surviving, and that was good enough for him.

He passed a sleepless night, however, and heard the ship's bell ringing every half hour until finally Danvers came to wake him.

'Time to get up!' said Danvers. 'Mr Masters is lending us his boat. Simpson and his seconds are going in the captain's boat.'

Another shadowy figure appeared. 'A cold morning,' said Preston. 'I've brought you some tea.'

Hornblower drank the hot sweet tea gratefully. 'Give me another cup,' he said, and was proud that he could think of tea at that moment.

It was still dark as they jumped down into the boat and rowed towards the land. Danvers had a bottle of whisky and offered Hornblower some.

'No, thanks,' said Hornblower. The thought of drinking whisky on an empty stomach made him feel quite sick.

'The others have brought the doctor with them,' said Preston. 'But I don't suppose he'll be much use to anyone!' He laughed, then looked uncomfortably at Hornblower. 'How are you feeling?' he asked.

'Well enough,' said Hornblower. He was glad it was,

dark; he did not want the others to see his white, worried face.

But Simpson, when they met him, looked worried too. Lieutenant Masters came forward and spoke to the two duellists.

'This is the moment,' he said, 'for you two to shake hands and forget your argument.'

'Has Mr Simpson offered to apologize?' asked Danvers. Masters shook his head.

'Then the duel must continue,' said Danvers. 'Mr Masters, here is a coin. Please throw it, and the winner shall choose his weapon.'

'Very well,' said Masters. 'Heads or tails, Mr Hornblower?'

'Tails,' said Hornblower.

Masters threw the coin, caught it and held it up. 'Tails,' he said. 'Please choose your weapon, Mr Hornblower.'

He held out the two pistols: death in one hand, life in the other. Hornblower had an even chance. He took the left-hand pistol. The weapon felt icy cold in his hand.

Simpson took the other pistol and they stood face to face.

'For the last time,' said Masters loudly, 'cannot you two forget your argument?'

In the silence that followed, Hornblower was sure the others must hear the desperate beating of his heart.

'Very well then,' said Masters. 'Aim your weapons!'

Hornblower looked past Simpson at the grey sky. In a

moment, he thought, one of us will be dead.

'I shall say, "One, two, three, fire!"' said Masters. 'Are you ready?'

'Yes,' came Simpson's voice.

'Yes,' said Hornblower.

'One,' said Masters. Hornblower felt Simpson's pistol against his chest. He lifted his own weapon.

'Two,' said Masters.

Suddenly Hornblower knew that he could not kill Simpson. He lifted his pistol higher, until it was touching the top of Simpson's shoulder. A small wound would be enough – if his pistol was the loaded one.

'Three. Fire!' said Masters.

Hornblower fired. There was a small cloud of smoke, but no bang. This is death, he thought. My weapon was the unloaded one. A tenth of a second later there was another small cloud of smoke from Simpson's pistol. They both stood straight and still, not realizing what had happened.

'A miss-fire!' said Danvers. All four seconds hurried up to the duellists.

'Give me those pistols,' said Masters.

'Which one was loaded?' asked Hether.

'It is better not to know,' said Masters. 'Now, you two – you have both behaved bravely, and we can consider this argument finished.'

And so both midshipmen survived their duel, and

Hornblower fired. There was a small cloud of smoke, but no bang.
This is death, he thought.

Hornblower became famous for his coolness instead of his seasickness. But other stories about the duel were whispered too. Hornblower heard them, and suspected that someone had cheated him. Some days later he asked to see the captain.

'Send him in,' said Keene tiredly. A very angry young man came into the cabin.

'I can guess what you're going to say,' said Keene.

'Sir – neither of those pistols was loaded!'

'That's right,' said Keene.

'That was unfair of you, sir! You have made me look a fool and . . .'

'Mr Hornblower, please control yourself,' said Keene. 'I have saved two lives, and you and Mr Simpson have both proved that you are brave men. Some advice for you – don't fight any more duels. Men who are always fighting duels are never good officers, and never popular ones either. Now, listen to me. Captain Pellew of the *Indefatigable* wants another midshipman – and one who can play whist. He would like to have you.'

Pellew! Hornblower had heard about him. His midshipmen could expect excitement, promotion, prize money. This was his big chance.

'That is very good of you, sir,' said Hornblower. 'I don't know how to thank you. But you accepted me as your midshipman here, and of course I must stay with you.'

The grey, sick face smiled. 'Thank you, Hornblower. I

shall always remember that. But I shall not live much longer. And this ship is no place for you. You are an able young man and you must have your chance of promotion. You will accept Captain Pellew's invitation – and I shall have a quieter life.'

'Aye, aye, sir,' said Hornblower.

2

The Cargo of Rice

In the Bay of Biscay the sea was covered with white sails. A large number of French cargo ships were desperately trying to escape from the English frigate *Indefatigable*. The French warships which were supposed to guard these cargo ships were further out in the Atlantic, hundreds of miles away. They were fighting a terrible battle with the English fleet for the control of the sea. Meanwhile, here in the Bay of Biscay, the *Indefatigable* was taking advantage of the warships' absence to chase and catch the slow-moving cargo ships. They were full of food for the hungry French people, and would make valuable prizes for the English King.

Ship after ship was caught. Small crews of four or five men then took command of each cargo ship and sailed it to England, while the frigate hurried to take another prize.

On the deck of the *Indefatigable* Captain Pellew watched impatiently as one of the big cargo ships tried desperately to escape.

'Get ready to fire!' said Captain Pellew.

The gunners turned their big guns towards the cargo ship.

'Fire high!' ordered Pellew. 'Damage her sails!'

Several heavy cannon balls crashed into the cargo ship.

That was enough. Her flag was lowered, and Pellew brought his big frigate closer.

'What's your name?' he shouted across the rough grey sea.

'*Marie Galante*,' came the answer. 'With a cargo of rice from New Orleans.'

'Rice!' said Pellew. 'That's a fine cargo. I need a prize crew to sail her home.' He saw Hornblower standing hopefully beside him. 'Mr Hornblower!'

'Sir!'

'Take four seamen. Sail that ship to England and wait there for orders.'

'Aye, aye, sir.'

One of the ship's boats was already in the water, waiting to take the next prize crew. Hornblower looked down at the boat. It was a long jump, but Pellew was impatient and there was no time to lose. Hornblower jumped.

He landed on the edge of the boat. For one long, frightening second he thought he was going to fall backwards into the sea, but a seaman caught him and pulled him into the boat.

'Thank you,' said Hornblower. He asked the lieutenant in command of the boat to take him to the *Marie Galante*. The lieutenant gave him four experienced seamen.

'Keep them away from strong drink,' he advised Hornblower. 'And watch the French crew. If they

'Marie Galante', *came the answer. 'With a cargo of rice from New Orleans.'*

possibly can, they'll retake the ship and put you in a French prison.'

They reached the big cargo ship and climbed up the side. The first thing Hornblower saw when he reached the deck was a Frenchman holding an empty bottle. 'English dogs,' said the Frenchman thickly, and sat down heavily on the deck. It was clear that the other French seamen had also been drinking, and there was a half-empty box of wine bottles on the deck. One of Hornblower's seamen picked up a bottle.

'Put that down!' ordered Hornblower. His voice sounded very young. The seaman hesitated. 'Put it down!' said Hornblower again, desperate with worry. He knew that he had to make the seaman obey him. He stared angrily at the man and his hand moved towards his pistol. The seaman put the bottle back in the box.

'Take the prisoners,' ordered Hornblower, 'and lock them up.'

Hornblower himself threw the bottles into the sea. Then he turned to the problem of repairing the damaged sails.

It really was not too difficult. His crew were all experienced seamen and, after the first difficult moment with the wine bottles, they obeyed his orders happily enough.

While his seamen were repairing the damage to the sails, Hornblower went to the captain's cabin and studied the ship's position on the map. He had already learnt how to do this, but he had never done it for a real ship before. He checked his mathematics twice, then went up on deck again.

'Steer north-east,' he told the man at the wheel.

'North-east,' repeated the seaman. 'Aye, aye, sir.'

They were three hundred miles from England. Two days with a good wind – but how long if the wind changed?

There was so much to do and think about – and only four men and himself to get the ship to England. Hornblower walked restlessly up and down the deck, as darkness fell.

'Why don't you get some sleep, sir?' asked the man at the wheel.

'I will, later on,' answered Hornblower, although the thought of sleep had never entered his head.

He knew it was good advice, and he actually went to the captain's cabin and lay down, but he could not sleep. Then he remembered something else and hurried up on deck again.

'We haven't checked the hold to see if the ship is taking in water,' he said to Matthews, the oldest seaman.

'No, sir,' agreed Matthews.

'Let's do it now,' said Hornblower. Matthews fetched a light and together they opened the door to the hold and threw down a long stick on a rope. When they heard the stick hit the bottom, they pulled the rope up, and to Hornblower's surprise the stick came up dry.

This was very unusual. All ships took in some water. And surely a cannon ball from the frigate had hit the *Marie Galante.*

Just then, however, the wind changed, and now began to blow them away from England. At once Hornblower was busy with the problem of keeping the cargo ship away from the dangerous rocks near the French coast. There was no longer any chance of reaching England in two days – and there was no chance of any sleep for Hornblower that night.

Early the next morning the French captain asked to speak with Hornblower. In his boyhood Hornblower had received French, music and dancing lessons from a French teacher. The unfortunate teacher had soon discovered that Hornblower had no ear for music at all, which of course made it impossible to teach him to dance. The teacher therefore spent all his time teaching his pupil French. Now these lessons were unexpectedly useful. Hornblower was shy at first, but his French was much better than the captain's English, and he soon became more confident.

'My men are hungry,' said the captain. 'And I have a cook.'

They made an agreement. The French seamen promised that they would not try to retake the ship, and they were allowed on deck while their cook prepared a hot meal for everyone.

'This wind is no good for you,' said the French captain.

'That's right,' said Hornblower coldly. He did not want this Frenchman to realize how worried he was.

'The ship is moving a little heavily,' said the captain.

'Perhaps,' said Hornblower.

'Is the ship taking in water?'

'No,' said Hornblower. 'The hold was dry when we checked last night.'

'Ah,' said the captain, 'that is natural. We are carrying a cargo of rice, remember.'

Hornblower understood at once. Rice takes in water, he thought miserably. Why didn't I realize that before?

'A cannon ball from your frigate hit the ship's side,' continued the captain. 'Of course you have checked the damage?'

'Of course,' lied Hornblower bravely.

As soon as he could, he spoke privately with Matthews.

'I'll go over the ship's side and take a look, sir,' said Matthews. Hornblower was about to agree. Then he shook his head.

'I'll go over the side myself,' he said.

Afterwards he was not sure why he had said this. There were two probable reasons, however. First, he remembered Captain Pellew's words. 'Never', the captain had told his midshipmen, 'order your men to do anything that you aren't ready to do yourself.' The second reason was one of responsibility. This is my fault, Hornblower said to himself. It's my problem now.

The seamen tied a rope around his waist and pulled

him slowly along through the icy grey water. He could not see any holes. The seamen pulled him up again onto the deck and he went over and checked the other side.

This time he found a hold just below the waterline. It was half a metre across, and taking in water fast. Hornblower thought of all the water that had entered the ship since the ball hit it, and he felt sick and miserable.

He gave orders to his men to cover the hole with a sail. The French seamen helped too. Although it was no longer their ship, they did not want to drown. The French captain watched them work.

'I spent five years in a prison ship in Portsmouth during the last war,' he said to Hornblower.

'Yes,' said Hornblower impatiently. He was sorry for the French captain, but he was very worried, and aching with cold. He went down to the cabin and changed into dry clothes. As he did so, he heard worrying noises from the cargo in the hold.

He came back on deck and went over to see how his men were getting on with covering the hole. Just then, however, one of the French seamen pointed to the deck.

For a few seconds Hornblower stared too, without seeing anything. Then he noticed that cracks were appearing between the wooden boards of the deck. The French captain stared at the cracks too.

'*Le riz!*' he said excitedly to Hornblower. 'The – the rice! The cargo – it is getting bigger!'

'That's it, sir!' shouted Matthews in alarm. 'The

'The rice will get bigger and bigger until it opens the ship up,'
shouted Matthews.

water's got into the hold and into the rice too. The rice will get bigger and bigger until it opens the ship up. The cracks between the boards will get wider, and the water will come in—'

Hornblower tried hard to seem calm. 'Then we must cover that hole as quickly as possible,' he said. 'Hurry, you men.'

At last the sail was in place over the hole, but alarming noises still came from every part of the ship as the rice began to open up new cracks everywhere.

Cold and stupid from sleeplessness, Hornblower stood there on deck, worrying and wondering. Then he saw a small grey shape running along the deck. It was followed by another, and another.

'Rats!' shouted Matthews. 'It must be really bad down there in the hold!'

Rats! The ship was carrying a cargo of rice. With plenty of food the rats would not normally leave their home – unless something was terribly wrong down there.

'We'll throw the rice out,' decided Hornblower. But that was not easy. The bags of rice were packed closely together. Lifting them out of the hold was a back-breakingly difficult job. One by one the seamen lifted the bags up on deck and threw them into the hungry sea. But it was no good.

'The ship's lower in the water, sir,' said Matthews sadly. He was right – and this was after hundreds of bags of rice had been thrown out.

'Prepare to abandon ship, Matthews,' said Hornblower bravely. He was near to tears, but he would not allow either the Frenchmen or his own seamen to guess that.

'Aye, aye, sir,' said Matthews.

The seamen stopped working in the hold and hurried to put food and water in the ship's boat.

'Excuse me, sir,' said Matthews, 'but you'll need warm clothes. I once spent ten days in an open boat.'

'Thank you, Matthews,' said Hornblower. He fetched the map from the cabin too. He looked doubtfully at the boat, which did not seem big enough for seventeen men – twelve Frenchmen and his own crew.

They let the boat down into the water. As they did so, a tearing crash from the hold informed them that the cargo was still growing. There was not a moment to lose.

The ship was so low in the water that it was quite easy for Hornblower to step down into the boat. His own crew made room for him. They rowed slowly away from the ship, which was going down fast.

Hornblower watched as a big wave broke over the *Marie Galante's* deck. She shook a little, then the hungry waters closed over her and she disappeared for ever.

'She's gone,' said Matthews.

She's gone, thought Hornblower, and it was all my fault. He stared very hard at the sun, hoping that nobody would notice the tears in his eyes.

The boat was small and crowded, and they spent a cold,

miserable night. When the sun came up the next morning, Hornblower realized that the wind had changed, so he ordered the men to put up the boat's small sail.

'Steer north by north-east,' he told Matthews.

'Aye, aye, sir.'

But the French captain began waving his arms about. 'Sir,' he cried, 'this is madness. It will take us a week to reach England. We cannot survive so long in this small, crowded boat. What if a storm comes? Bordeaux is only a day away. We shall be safe there.'

'We are going to England,' said Hornblower. He pointed one of his pistols at the captain's chest. The captain stepped back at once. Hornblower passed another pistol to Matthews.

'Shoot any man who looks dangerous,' he said quietly.

'Aye, aye, sir,' replied Matthews.

All that day and all the following night they sailed slowly towards England. Hornblower even managed to sleep a little. But the next morning they saw a sail.

'What kind of ship is she, Matthews?' asked Hornblower.

'I don't like the look of her, sir,' replied the old seaman. 'She looks French to me. Possibly a privateer.'

They tried desperately to escape, but it was useless. The privateer was big and fast, with cannon that could blow their little boat out of the water. Soon Hornblower and his men were prisoners.

The privateer's captain received Hornblower politely. 'Welcome, sir, to the privateer *Pique*,' he said in French.

'I am Captain Neuville. And you . . .?'

'Midshipman Hornblower, of the frigate *Indefatigable*,' said Hornblower. He was angry and ashamed.

'Do not blame yourself,' said Neuville smoothly, 'for the fortunes of war . . . I am sure you find that pistol quite unnecessarily heavy. Please allow me to take care of it for you. And now let me show you your berth.'

It was two decks down, just below the water line. 'Our slave deck,' explained Neuville.

'Slave deck?' repeated Hornblower in surprise.

'Yes,' said Neuville carelessly. 'The slaves were kept here on the long voyage from Africa across the Atlantic. We can no longer make that voyage because of this unfortunate war, so now I have made my slave ship into a privateer . . . Here is your berth. If we have to fight, you will be locked in. At other times you are free to move about the ship. Do not, however, do anything to damage my ship in any way. If you try, my crew will simply drop you over the side into the sea.'

These coldly inhuman words filled Hornblower with alarm, but he kept his face expressionless. 'I understand,' he said calmly.

'Excellent! Now, is there anything you need, sir?'

Hornblower looked around the big, empty berth with its smoky lamp. 'May I have something to read?' he asked.

'Only a French book about mathematics for seamen,' answered Neuville. 'You are welcome to borrow that, if you think you can understand it.'

*Hornblower looked around the big, empty berth with
its smoky lamp.*

'I'll try,' said Hornblower.

He was glad to have something to keep him busy during the long, boring days while the privateer sailed in search of prizes. He was angry with himself, deeply ashamed and very lonely and miserable. He realized that nobody would punish him for his mistakes. Who could expect an inexperienced young midshipman to sail home a badly damaged ship, with a prize crew of only four? But Hornblower still blamed himself. The day of his eighteenth birthday was the worst day of all. Eighteen, and a prisoner in a French privateer! He hated himself.

The privateer sailed backwards and forwards in search of prizes. Then one morning the French seamen saw a sail. It belonged to a large ship, which came quickly towards the privateer. That meant only one thing – a warship.

Hope rose in Hornblower's heart. England controlled the seas. The warship, if it was a warship, was probably English. He looked at Neuville, trying to read his thoughts. The *Pique* was fast enough to escape quite easily. But perhaps the strange ship was not a ship of war at all. The big cargo ships of the East India Company looked very similar to English warships. Perhaps this ship *was* one of the Company's cargo ships and hoped that her warlike looks would frighten the privateer away.

Suddenly Matthews appeared on deck, wildly excited. 'That's the old *Indefatigable*, sir, I'm sure of it!'

Neuville turned to Hornblower. 'Your ship, I believe, Mr Hornblower?'

'Yes.'

'I'm afraid you will never see her again. No frigate can catch my ship. You will soon see that for yourself.'

Hornblower did not answer. He went down to his berth. He was homesick, desperately homesick for the *Indefatigable* with its dark, airless midshipmen's berth, the smells, the uneatable food.

The slave deck was empty, as all the seamen were busy on deck. In the lamplight Hornblower looked at his bed with the mathematics book beside it. Nearby was a locked door. Behind it, Hornblower knew, were pots of paint. I wonder, thought Hornblower, if I could start a fire in there! But the door was thick and very strong and its lock was excellent. Suddenly Hornblower had an idea. He picked up the book and started to pull the pages out of it. He made them into little balls and threw them on the floor. Carefully he covered them with hot oil from the lamp. He pulled the bedclothes off the bed, then he lit the paper with the lamp.

He climbed slowly up to the deck, leaving the door open. Fires need air, he said to himself. He walked slowly backwards and forwards, pretending to watch the *Indefatigable*, which was now a long way behind.

The wind was blowing strongly and the privateer was flying along. The French seamen went busily about their work, while Hornblower wondered what was happening below, on the slave deck.

Suddenly Hornblower saw smoke coming from below. A French seaman saw it too and gave the alarm. '*Au feu!*'

Wind, water and fire are the seaman's oldest enemies, thought Hornblower. But fire is the most terrible of all. A painted wooden sailing ship will burn like a match . . . Neuville gave Hornblower an angry, suspicious look as he hurried to organize the firefighters. The man at the wheel pointed towards the cabin window. Hornblower could see flames through the glass. At that moment the glass broke and the flames came through the opening. That paint must be burning nicely now, thought Hornblower calmly. Later, when he thought about that moment, he was surprised by his calmness.

All around him seamen were fighting the fire – and losing the battle. There was a noise from below as something exploded. Then the deck at Hornblower's feet seemed to open in a fiery red smile. One of the French officers began arguing with Neuville, who shook his head. Hornblower caught a few words of their conversation.

He understood the situation. The wind was carrying the *Pique* away from the frigate, but it was also blowing the fire all the way through the ship. While Neuville continued to sail away from the frigate, the fire would continue to destroy everything in its way. If he turned, the wind would blow the flames out over the sea, away from the front of the ship.

The fire was now getting out of control, and Neuville had to decide fast. Angrily, he gave orders to turn the ship into the wind – and to sail towards the English frigate.

The *Indefatigable* came flying towards the burning privateer. Two boats full of seamen rowed up, and an English officer stepped up on deck. It was Bolton, third lieutenant of the *Indefatigable*. He stared at Hornblower in surprise.

'What are YOU doing here?' he said, but he did not wait for an answer. He made Neuville his prisoner, then he and his men started work controlling the fire.

They succeeded, and the privateer survived. She was badly damaged, but a good prize crew could sail her safely to England to be repaired and sent to sea again.

Afterwards Captain Pellew called Hornblower into his cabin.

'Now, young Hornblower,' said Pellew, 'let's have your report.'

Hornblower told his story. Pellew did not blame him for losing the *Marie Galante*. 'You did your best,' he said. 'The important thing is this. The French needed her cargo, and you made sure they didn't get it.

'It's the same with the *Pique*. Oh, she's a valuable prize and I'm glad we've got her. But the most important thing is that she's no longer in French hands. She can't be a danger to English cargo ships again . . . It was lucky that she caught fire like that. Have you any idea how it happened, Mr Hornblower?'

The Indefatigable *came flying towards the burning privateer.*

Hornblower was ready for this question. Now is the time to answer truthfully, he thought. Captain Pellew will be pleased. Perhaps he will even make me an acting-lieutenant. But he does not know the full story of my mistakes on the *Marie Galante*.

'No, sir,' said Hornblower calmly. 'There was a lot of paint in a cupboard on the slave deck. Perhaps that caught fire. That's the only explanation I can think of.'

This answer was his punishment to himself for his carelessness. Now he could live at peace with himself again.

'All the same,' said Pellew, looking at Hornblower, 'it was very fortunate.'

3

The Spanish Galleys

As the months passed and the war continued, the old *Indefatigable* and her crew had many adventures. Hornblower survived all the dangers and was now a tough and experienced midshipman. The fortunes of war went first one way and then another, until Spain, which had been France's enemy, made peace with France.

The frigate was in the Bay of Cadiz at the time, and Hornblower was on deck when the news arrived.

'Boat coming, sir,' he reported to Lieutenant Soames. 'Eight oars, and flying a Spanish flag. There's an officer on board.'

Soames hurried to tell Captain Pellew, who arrived to meet his visitor. The Spanish captain bowed politely and offered him a letter.

'Here, Hornblower,' said Pellew, holding the letter unopened, 'speak French to him. Ask him to come to my cabin for a drink.'

But the Spaniard clearly wanted Pellew to open the letter at once. It was in French. Pellew handed it to Hornblower.

'Does this mean the Spaniards have made peace with the French?' Pellew asked.

Hornblower read the twelve lines of extremely polite French. 'That's right, sir,' he said.

But the Spanish captain had another message for Pellew. He spoke to Hornblower in French. 'Please tell your captain that Spain cannot allow the enemies of France to remain in Spanish waters. We must ask you to leave. In six hours from now' – he took out his watch – 'our cannon will have orders to fire on you.'

Hornblower explained this to Pellew. 'Tell him—' Pellew began angrily. Then he stopped. 'No, I won't let him see I'm angry. Say something polite to him – something about personal friendship in these troubled times.' He bowed to the Spanish captain, who took off his hat and bowed again.

As soon as the Spanish captain had left, Pellew gave orders to sail at once. Hornblower stood with Mr Wales the gunner, looking at the beautiful white houses of Cadiz.

'Hello!' said Wales. 'I see we've got company.'

Two long, narrow, brightly-painted galleys had appeared and were moving towards the *Indefatigable*. Hornblower watched their oars rising and falling like the wings of a sea bird. The effect was very beautiful. Up . . . forward . . . down . . . went the oars. At the front of each galley two long guns pointed towards the *Indefatigable*.

'Big guns, those,' said Wales. 'They can knock a ship to pieces in twenty minutes.'

As the galleys passed the *Indefatigable*, Hornblower noticed a strong smell, like the smell of farm animals. 'All galleys smell like that,' explained Wales. 'Fifty oars, with

The oars of the Spanish galleys rose and fell like the wings of a sea bird.

four men to every oar. Two hundred galley slaves, all tied to their seats. They're tied to their seats when they arrive, and they're never untied until they die. The crew don't do much cleaning – there aren't many of them, anyway.'

Hornblower, as usual, wanted exact information. 'How many are there in the crew, Mr Wales?'

'Thirty, perhaps. Enough to work the sails – or the guns. But that's why they never untie the slaves, of course. There are only thirty in the crew to control two hundred slaves.'

Soon the news came that Spain was actually at war with England. Most of the rest of Europe, exhausted by war, had already made peace with France. So England was now alone and friendless, and desperate for fresh food for her soldiers in Gibraltar. Now that Spain was an enemy, the English in Gibraltar had to buy bread and meat from North Africa, and the towns of Oran, Tetuan and Algiers all grew rich on British gold.

One hot, still day the *Indefatigable* was half-way between Oran and Gibraltar. Her job was to guard several food ships and their cargoes and bring them safely in to Gibraltar. But the sea was like a silver mirror and there was not a breath of wind. Captain Pellew had ordered the small boats from every ship into the water. The crews had to row the boats to pull the helpless sailing ships along. They moved desperately slowly – less than two kilometres an hour.

The *Indefatigable* was pulled along by her two biggest boats – the longboat and the cutter, which each held forty men. It was exhausting, back-breaking work and the men were so tired that at first they did not notice what was happening. Then they heard the voice of their captain.

'Mr Chadd! Mr Soames! Come at once and get pistols and cutlasses for your men. Here come our friends from Cadiz.'

Over the calm, flat sea, the two Spanish galleys were moving quickly towards the helpless ships. 'This is their chance, of course,' said Pellew angrily. 'They'll be able to row up to the cargo ships and attack them one by one – and without a wind we can't even get near enough to fire at them!'

The crews fetched their pistols and cutlasses and hurried back into their boats to attack the galleys.

'What do you think you're doing, Mr Hornblower?' shouted Pellew, as he saw him preparing the little jolly boat for battle. 'What do you think you can do with a four-metre boat and a crew of six against a war-galley?'

'We can row out to one of the cargo ships and help them, sir,' said Hornblower.

'Oh, very well then – just don't do anything stupid.'

And so the jolly boat rowed into battle.

'Good for you, Mr Hornblower!' said Able Seaman Jackson. 'I thought we were going to miss the fun!'

'Pull, you men! Pull!' Hornblower shouted as his

excited men rowed hard to catch up with the longboat and the cutter. He did not know what was going to happen, but he wanted to be part of the battle.

Then a terrible thing happened. One of the galleys turned until it was pointing straight at the cutter, and her oars began to move more quickly. Hornblower remembered his history lessons and how the Greeks and Romans used their war-galleys in battle. The galley was coming in to hit the cutter. He saw Lieutenant Soames in the cutter, wide-eyed with fear. Then, with a terrible noise of breaking wood, the galley's sharp metal front crashed into the side of the cutter and broke the boat into two pieces. Screams came from the wounded and drowning men.

A kind of fever, a fighting madness, filled Hornblower. The jolly boat was now very close to the back end of the galley.

'Throw the grapnel, Jackson!' he shouted. Jackson took the heavy metal grapnel on its long rope and threw it hard and straight. The grapnel caught on the painted wood along the galley's side. Now the galley was pulling the jolly boat along. A Spanish seaman came running along the galley's deck with a knife.

'He's going to cut the rope! Shoot him!' screamed Hornblower. There was a bang and the Spanish seaman fell to the deck. 'Pistols ready, boys!' ordered Hornblower.

Several faces appeared along the galley's side, and guns pointed down into the jolly boat. Shots were fired. One

'He's going to cut the rope! Shoot him!' screamed Hornblower.

man in the boat was wounded, but the faces disappeared. 'Reload pistols!' ordered Hornblower, shaking with excitement and fighting madness.

The glass of the galley's cabin window above them broke with a crash and a gun pointed through it. Without thinking, Hornblower fired his pistol again. Then he took hold of the grapnel rope. 'I'm going up! Follow me one at a time!' he ordered. Then he threw himself at the grapnel rope and climbed up towards the cabin window.

His feet found the window; he kicked out the rest of the glass and threw himself through into the cabin. At his feet lay a dead man. He opened the cabin door and found himself on a small deck. In front of him were the galley slaves. He saw the sea of bearded faces and sunburned bodies, moving backwards and forwards as they rowed. A man with a whip was shouting orders in Spanish.

Hornblower looked past the slaves to the Spanish seamen standing by the two big cannon at the front of the galley. There were not enough seamen to fire them. Clearly, half the crew had left their guns when Hornblower's jolly boat attacked.

He heard a footstep behind him – but it was only Jackson. 'Oldroyd's coming next,' he said. 'Franklin's dead.'

Beside them a ladder led to the top deck. At that moment Oldroyd appeared. 'Follow me,' said Hornblower.

There were about twelve Spaniards on the small top deck, but two were dead, one was wounded and two were busy at the wheel, steering the galley. The others were staring down at the jolly boat. Hornblower was still feverish with excitement. He jumped up onto the deck, screaming like a madman. He fired his pistol into the face of one Spanish seaman, then buried his cutlass in the body of another. Jackson was beside him with his cutlass.

'Kill them! Kill them!' screamed Jackson as his cutlass whistled down. Another pistol crashed – that was Oldroyd – and then, unbelievably, the fight on the upper deck was over. Hornblower never knew how they did it. Perhaps the Spaniards had never expected three men to be stupid enough to attack twelve. Perhaps they had expected the man in the cabin below to warn them if any attacker came that way.

The deck was covered with dead and wounded men. One tried to get up. Before Hornblower could stop them, Jackson and Oldroyd picked him up and threw him over the ship's side. They picked up another wounded man.

'Stop that!' shouted Hornblower. The two seamen dropped the man on the deck with a crash and stared at him stupidly. 'Come on,' ordered Hornblower. 'We've got work to do.'

He pointed to the Spaniards at the front end of the ship, beside the guns. As Hornblower came forward, one of them fired a pistol, but missed. Down below the slaves were still working at their oars while the man with the whip shouted his orders.

'Stop!' shouted Hornblower. But the slaves continued

rowing. Jackson pointed his pistol at the nearest slave. But Hornblower was sick of killing. 'No, Jackson,' he ordered. 'Reload my pistols for me.'

He stood at the top of the ladder like a man in a dream. The galley slaves were still rowing. His enemies – about twelve of them – were still standing at the other end of the galley, thirty metres away. Behind him the wounded men were screaming. How could he stop the rowers?

'I'll take down the flag,' said Oldroyd at last.

'Yes, that's right,' said Hornblower. The red and yellow Spanish flag came down. Until then Hornblower did not realize that nobody was steering the galley. 'Take the wheel, Oldroyd,' he ordered.

A pistol ball whistled past his head, but Hornblower did not notice it. He was staring out to sea. There were the cargo ships; there was the *Indefatigable*. Were any of the frigate's boats nearby? Yes – the captain's private boat was about four hundred metres away. The seamen in it were standing up and waving. That's because we took down the Spanish flag, thought Hornblower. He hoped they realized that he still needed help.

'Steer towards the captain's boat, Oldroyd,' he ordered.

Another pistol crashed. This is no good, thought Hornblower. The Spanish crew up at the front by the guns could still attack them, and retake the galley. He had to do something.

His fighting madness had left him. He did not care what happened to him now; he felt neither hope nor fear.

'Give me my pistols, Jackson,' he ordered. 'Stay at the wheel, Oldroyd. Jackson, follow me. Don't do anything unless I say.'

With one pistol in his hand he went down the ladder, along the slave deck and up the ladder towards the Spaniards. They stared at him in fear and surprise. Two steps from the group Hornblower stopped and pointed.

'Drop your weapons, all of you,' he ordered. 'You are my prisoners.' The Spaniards did not move and continued to stare at him like men in a dream. Only one man made a small movement. Hornblower stared angrily at him. Then, one by one, the pistols and cutlasses fell to the deck. 'Jackson, guard them,' ordered Hornblower. He now turned to the man with the whip.

'Stop the rowers,' he ordered, pointing to the slaves. The man with the whip stared at him disbelievingly. 'Stop them, I say,' said Hornblower, lifting his pistol. That was enough. The man shouted an order and the oars were still.

Hornblower turned back to shout to Oldroyd at the other end of the galley. 'Where's the captain's boat now?'

'Three hundred metres, sir.'

How long would the captain's boat take to cover three hundred metres? And, before it arrived, would the Spaniards come out of their dream and fight? Hornblower fought hard to keep his self-control. The next few minutes seemed like an hour.

'Welcome, sir,' said Hornblower to Lieutenant Chadd.

'Stop the rowers,' ordered Hornblower, lifting his pistol.

'The galley is ours, but we need to tie up these prisoners. I think I have done everything else.'

Now he felt dull and stupid. In a dream, he heard the happy shouts of the *Indefatigable's* crew as the frigate came up to the galley. He was still in a dream when he made his report to Captain Pellew, but he remembered to tell him how brave Jackson and Oldroyd had been.

'Well done, Hornblower,' said the captain. 'Poor Soames was killed in the cutter and I need another lieutenant now. I'm thinking of making you an acting-lieutenant, Hornblower.'

Hornblower still felt stupid. Fighting madness, he thought, has won me this promise of promotion. It was wild, black hate that made me attack that galley. I was lucky to survive – and I must remember that.

'Thank you, sir,' he said aloud.

4

The Duchess and
the Devil

Many months later, Acting-Lieutenant Hornblower was sailing *Le Rêve* into Gibraltar Bay. The little French ship had been taken as a prize by the frigate *Indefatigable*. Hornblower was in command of the ship and Jackson – now a Leading Seaman – was steering. Hornblower felt that the whole English fleet was watching as he sailed between the big warships and arrived at last in the bay. Ten minutes later he was reporting his arrival to the Admiral.

'You say *Le Rêve*'s fast?' said the Admiral. 'Then I'll buy her. We need ships like her to carry despatches. In fact I need one now. You can sail her to England as soon as my despatches are ready. Meanwhile, will you come to dinner at Admiralty House tonight?'

Hornblower was pleased and excited by the Admiral's first order. It was a chance of independent command and a chance to see England again, which he had not seen for three years. The second piece of news was less welcome, however. Hornblower had to spend a long time brushing his uniform and shining his shoes.

There were many people at the dinner at Admiralty House. To his surprise, Hornblower was introduced to one of the most important visitors – a duchess.

'This is Mr Hornblower, the new captain of *Le Rêve*.

Mr Hornblower – the Duchess of Wharfedale,' said the Admiral's wife.

Hornblower bowed politely. The duchess had fearless blue eyes in a middle-aged face, which had once been very beautiful.

'So this is the young man, eh?' said the duchess. 'A bit young to command a ship, isn't 'e?'

She certainly doesn't sound like a duchess, thought Hornblower in surprise. He put one hand on his heart and bowed again, as his French teacher had taught him.

'Oo, you do look funny!' cried the duchess. She too put her hand on her heart and bowed. Everyone laughed. Fortunately, the dinner bell rang soon afterwards and Hornblower could sit in peace at the end of the long dinner table with the youngest and least important officers.

'You're going to have an amusing travelling companion,' a young army captain said to Hornblower.

'Travelling companion?' repeated Hornblower in surprise.

'Hasn't anyone told you? When you sail tomorrow with the Admiral's despatches, you will also take the Duchess of Wharfedale to England.'

'My goodness!' said Hornblower weakly. 'But who *is* she? She doesn't talk like a duchess – or behave like one either.'

'No – her husband was old and sick when he married her. Her friends say she kept a pub. You can imagine what her enemies say.'

'*When you sail tomorrow with the Admiral's despatches, you will also take the Duchess of Wharfedale to England.*'

'But what is she doing here?'

'She's on her way back to England. She was in Italy when the French army marched in. She escaped by ship to Gibraltar. And of course the Admiral wants to do his best for her. After all, she is a duchess now, even if she kept a pub before.' The duchess's loud laugh rang out from the top end of the table. 'I'm sure she'll keep you amused,' said the young captain. 'May I pass you the vegetables?'

Hornblower did not worry too much about the duchess. He was too busy preparing his ship. She had only four small guns to fight off her enemies, which meant she was safe from no one. Even the smallest cargo ship had bigger guns than that. If *Le Rêve* was attacked, the only thing to do was run away. So Hornblower very carefully checked all the sails and made sure that everyone in his eleven-man crew knew his job. Then he put on his best uniform and prepared to welcome the duchess on board.

The duchess was helped on board. Jackson showed her the small cabin while Hornblower accepted the two heavy packets of despatches. Then they were ready to sail.

It was stormy when they left Gibraltar Bay. Hornblower was too busy to worry about the Duchess. He had to watch out for French and Spanish warships and privateers. After eleven hours he was passing Cape Trafalgar – and feeling hungry. It was pleasant to be a captain and to order dinner when he wanted it.

He sent the cook to knock on the duchess's cabin door. But the duchess was too seasick to eat. Hornblower did not care. He ate hungrily, then went up on deck again as night fell.

'It's getting very foggy, sir,' Midshipman Winyatt reported.

'It'll be really thick by morning,' said Hornblower. He looked again at the map. 'We'll have to steer west instead of north-west. We want to keep a long way away from Cape St Vincent.'

A very small thing can change a person's whole life. Afterwards Hornblower had plenty of time to think about that. During the night he was often up on deck; but he was resting in his cabin when the alarm call came. He hurried up on deck at once.

The first light of day was shining dully through the thick blanket of fog. There was very little wind. Jackson was steering. 'Listen, sir!' he whispered.

Hornblower listened. At first he heard only the usual everyday sounds of his own ship. Then he heard the sounds of another ship. 'There's a ship close to us,' he whispered.

'Yes, sir – and after I sent for you, I heard someone giving an order in Spanish.'

'Call "All hands", but do it quietly,' ordered Hornblower. But he knew it was no use. He could call his men and load his guns, but what could he do against a warship?

'Good morning, young man!' said a voice behind him. He jumped with surprise. He had actually forgotten about the duchess.

'Stop that noise!' he whispered angrily to her.

Through the fog he could hear Spanish voices, then the sound of a ship's bell. And immediately, from all around them, other bells answered.

'My God!' whispered Jackson. 'We're in the middle of an enemy fleet!'

'They won't see us if the fog stays down,' said Winyatt hopefully.

'But the fog won't stay down,' said Hornblower impatiently. 'When the sun rises, the fog will lift.'

Hornblower took a heavy metal bar and began to tie it to the despatches.

'Please,' said the duchess, 'what are you doing?'

'I'm going to throw these despatches into the sea,' explained Hornblower.

'Then they'll be lost for ever?'

'That's better than letting the Spaniards get them,' said Hornblower as patiently as he could.

'Let me look after them for you,' said the duchess.

'They'll probably search your bags, my lady.'

'My bags! I'll carry those despatches next to my skin! They'll never find them.'

Hornblower realized that the duchess was right.

'If they take us prisoner,' continued the duchess, 'I promise I won't tell anyone about those despatches, not until I can give them to a King's officer.'

'The fog's getting thinner already, sir,' said Jackson.

'Quick!' said the duchess. 'There's no time to lose.'

Hornblower handed her the despatches and turned away while she fastened them under the wide skirts of her fashionable dress. 'You can look now,' she said. 'I look a little fatter than before, but that isn't important.'

A watery sun was beginning to break through the fog now. With every second it was growing brighter. And then suddenly, the sea was covered with ships. There were four warships and two big frigates. All carried the red and yellow flag of Spain, and all were sailing towards them.

'Turn the ship,' ordered Hornblower. 'Steer back into the fog behind us. Perhaps we can get away from them.'

There was a crash of gunfire. A cannon ball hit the water beside them.

'My lady,' said Hornblower, 'that wasn't a warning shot. You must go to your cabin. It isn't safe for you here on deck.'

'No, no!' cried the duchess. 'Not in that airless box. I'd rather die.'

'Sail ahead!' called a seaman.

In the fog in front of them, the shape of another Spanish warship was beginning to appear. Escape was impossible.

Then two cannon balls from one of the warships

behind them hit the little ship with a crash like the end of the world. One ball hit the ship's side. The other hit her mast. Down fell the mast, with all the sails. Now *Le Rêve* was helpless.

'Is anybody hurt?' called Hornblower.

'Nothing serious, sir,' said one voice. Hornblower was surprised that anyone had survived.

'Check the hold to see if we're taking in water,' ordered Hornblower. Then he added, 'No – don't do that. If the Spaniards want to save this ship, let them do the work.' He turned to the duchess. 'You'd better go and pack your bags. I hope the Spaniards will make you comfortable.'

He was trying desperately hard to speak calmly. But the duchess knew what was going through his mind.

'Please, sir,' said Jackson. 'We can fight them. We can load our guns, and fire at them when they send their boats.' Hornblower pointed wordlessly to the seven Spanish ships. 'You're right, sir,' said Jackson softly. 'We haven't a chance.' A boat from one of the Spanish frigates was now coming towards them.

'A private word with you, please, Mr Hornblower,' said the duchess suddenly. Jackson and Winyatt moved away politely.

'Listen,' said the duchess quickly, looking straight at Hornblower. 'I'm not a duchess.'

'Good God!' said Hornblower. 'Who are you then?'

'Kitty Cobham. I am – I was a famous actress.' Quickly she told her story. 'I was caught in Italy when the

One cannon ball hit the ship's side. The other hit her mast.

French army marched in. I needed help, so I decided to be a duchess. I know about the Duchess of Wharfedale. I knew the Admiral at Gibraltar would help a duchess, although he would never lift a finger for an actress.'

'Give me back the despatches!' cried Hornblower. 'Quick!'

'If you want . . . but I can still be a duchess when the Spaniards come. They won't keep me a prisoner for long. They'll let me go in a month, and I'll guard those despatches, I promise! Please believe me . . . I've done a lot of bad things in my life. Now let me do something for my country.'

It was a strange thing for a man of nineteen to have to decide. Meanwhile, the Spaniards were throwing a grapnel. In a few seconds they would be on the deck. 'Keep the despatches,' said Hornblower at last. 'Hand them over when you can.'

He turned away to meet the Spanish lieutenant who was coming towards him. He introduced him to the duchess. The lieutenant bowed most politely and offered the duchess his hand. The duchess looked at him coldly and proudly. She was right, Hornblower realized. The despatches would be safe with her.

The Spaniards took Hornblower to a prison in the Spanish town of Ferrol. The prison itself was no worse than the midshipmen's berth, and the food and water were better. But he had lost his freedom, and he was deeply unhappy.

It was four months before he received any letters from England, but the first letter brought him some comfort in his misery.

'Dearest Boy,' it began. 'I hope it will give you happiness to hear that I took good care of the packets you gave me. They told me, when I handed them over, that you were a prisoner. My heart bleeds for you. They also told me that the Admiral was pleased with you . . . I think about you every day. Your good friend, Kitty Cobham.'

The same day the Spanish captain sent for Hornblower.

'Good afternoon,' he said politely.

'Good afternoon, sir,' said Hornblower. He was learning Spanish slowly and painfully.

'I have received news of your promotion,' said the Spanish captain. 'Here is the letter from the English Admiral. Because of your bravery you are now a full lieutenant. You will move into the officers' side of the prison. You will receive a lieutenant's half-pay and you will be free to go out for two hours every day if you give your parole.'

'Thank you,' said Hornblower.

During the long months that followed, those two hours became very important to Hornblower. Officers on parole were free for two hours each day. They were free to walk in the town, to buy a cup of chocolate or a glass of beer, to practise their Spanish on the soldiers and seamen there. But usually Hornblower preferred to spend his two hours near the sea.

One stormy day he was on the hill above Ferrol harbour, looking out to sea. The wind was so strong that he had difficulty in standing up straight. But he stayed outside, enjoying his freedom. He had been a prisoner for nearly two years, and for twenty-two hours every day he was locked in a small room with five other officers. So these two hours outside were important to him. He always watched the ships out at sea, and whenever an English ship sailed by, Hornblower stared at it like a thirsty man staring at a cup of water.

Today the sea was very rough. Hornblower could see the waves breaking on the cruel rocks that the local people called the Devil's Teeth. He was not alone on the hill. A Spanish guard was standing not far away, looking out to sea through his telescope. Suddenly the guard called out excitedly and several other soldiers came running. The guard had seen a ship, and soon Hornblower saw it too – a small grey sail. But why were the soldiers so excited?

'Please,' said Hornblower in his slow, careful Spanish, 'what can you see?'

The guard passed Hornblower his telescope, and through it Hornblower could see a second sail. The first ship, which looked like a Spanish privateer, was being chased by an English frigate. Would the Spanish ship reach the harbour with its big cannon before the English ship could catch her?

The guard saw the look on Hornblower's face and took his telescope away again. Along came an officer on a horse. He shouted an order and his men hurried to load the big cannon. If the English ship came near the coast, those guns would blow her out of the water.

Hornblower could see the two ships now without a telescope. Then the captain came along on his horse and Hornblower went up to him. He had to shout above the screaming of the wind.

'Sir, my parole finishes in ten minutes. Please may I stay?'

'Yes, stay,' replied the captain generously.

Excitedly, Hornblower watched the frigate chasing the privateer. The privateer was eight hundred metres ahead of the frigate – was she going to escape? Then suddenly a hole appeared in her mainsail. At once the wind blew the whole sail away. The Spanish privateer turned helplessly – and drove straight onto the Devil's Teeth.

At first the ship was hidden by the waves. Then Hornblower saw her, broken and mastless. There were men still alive on her decks. But how long could they live in those terrible waves? A crowd of townspeople and fishermen were watching now, but nobody was doing anything to save the men. Hornblower thought quickly. He ran up to the captain.

'Sir,' he said, 'let me try to save them. Perhaps some of the fishermen will come with me.'

Down in Ferrol harbour, Hornblower and six strong

Spanish fishermen were soon climbing into a small boat. The captain shouted to Hornblower.

'Remember I have your parole!'

'You have my parole, sir,' agreed Hornblower. For a few wonderful moments he had actually forgotten that he was a prisoner.

The fishermen rowed strongly through the mountainous waves towards the privateer, while the wind screamed like a wild animal in pain. Hornblower steered carefully, turning to meet the waves. Through the rain and sea-water he could see the men on the ship's deck. One of the men saw him and waved an arm. But there were only four survivors. Four, from a crew of twenty!

Hornblower steered the boat as close to the ship as he could. One survivor jumped and landed in the boat. Another survivor jumped and landed safely. The third was not so fortunate. He misjudged his jump, and landed in the sea. He disappeared at once beneath the angry waves and no one ever saw him again – but there was no time for sadness. The fourth survivor saw his chance and jumped safely into the boat.

'Any more?' shouted Hornblower. The last survivor shook his head. 'Let's go then.'

But now it was getting dark, and the men at the oars were too tired to row much further.

'It's too dangerous to try to get back to the harbour in the dark,' said Hornblower. 'We must get out to sea, away from all these rocks.'

Through the rain and sea-water Hornblower could see the men on the ship's deck.

The fishermen agreed with him, and they prepared for a night in an open boat. Hornblower realized that he was wet to the skin. He, the fishermen and the three survivors lay close together in the bottom of the boat and tried to keep warm. It was a long, uncomfortable night and they were all very cold and exhausted. But at last the sky grew lighter. One of the fishermen sat up and pointed.

'The English frigate!' he shouted.

Shaking with cold, Hornblower took off his shirt and waved it. The frigate sent a boat across, and the English seamen helped them all into it.

'I am a King's officer,' said Hornblower when he arrived on the deck of the frigate. 'May I speak to your captain, please?'

Soon, wearing warm dry clothes, he was drinking hot whisky-and-water with Captain Crome of the frigate *Syrtis*. 'Those Spanish fishermen will make good seamen for our ships,' said Crome.

'Sir,' said Hornblower, 'they came to sea to save lives. They are not prisoners of war.'

Crome stared at him coldly. Young lieutenants did not usually tell captains what to do. 'Are you telling me my job, sir?' he said.

'Oh no, sir, it's a long time since I read the Admiral's orders . . . I may be wrong.'

'Admiral's orders?' repeated Crome, in a different voice.

'Yes, sir. I think the orders say the same thing about

survivors too, sir – but I expect I'm wrong.'

'Oh, very well, Hornblower. I'll send them home. And now, what about you? You say you're a lieutenant. I can use you on this ship until we meet the Admiral again. Then he can decide what to do with you.'

The devil came to Hornblower that day in Crome's cabin. The devil offered him the thing he wanted most in the whole world. To eat salt meat and hard bread, to feel a ship's deck under his feet. To talk English again – to be free, free, free! But he had given his promise not to break parole . . . Before he had taken his next mouthful of whisky-and-water, Hornblower had defeated the devil.

'I gave my parole to the Spanish, sir.'

'You promised not to try to escape, then?'

Hornblower looked round the homely cabin, and his heart was breaking. 'Yes, sir. I must go back as soon as I can.'

'Have dinner with me and spend the night on the ship before you go,' said Crome. 'I'll send you all back to Ferrol as soon as the storm is over.'

Two days later, on a bright sunny morning, an English boat with a white flag sailed into Ferrol harbour. Ten men climbed out. Nine were laughing and shouting. The tenth man's face was expressionless. He did not smile even when the others put their arms around his shoulders.

Slowly the winter passed. It was almost spring when a Spanish soldier came to the prison and asked for

Hornblower. 'Please come with me. The captain has news for you.'

The captain smiled widely. 'This,' he said, waving a letter at Hornblower, 'is from the King of Spain. Because of your bravery in saving Spanish lives he is ordering me to give you your freedom.'

'Thank you, sir,' said Hornblower.

GLOSSARY

abandon   to leave a thing or a place (e.g. a sinking ship) and not plan to return

acting-   doing the job of another person for a time

admiral   the commander-in-chief of a country's warships

attack *(v)*   to start fighting or hurting somebody

aye aye   yes (used only by seamen in reply to an order)

bay *(n)*   an area of sea with land round three sides of it

berth   a place to sleep on a ship

bow *(v)*   to bend the head or body forward to show respect

cabin   a room on a ship

cannon   a large heavy gun which shoots metal balls

cargo   things that a ship carries

crack *(n)*   a thin, narrow hole

crew   all the people who work on a ship

cutlass   a weapon like a long knife, that sailors used to carry

cutter   a ship's boat that holds forty seamen

deck   the floor of a ship

despatches   official letters, reports, messages

devil   Satan, the enemy of God

duchess   a title for a woman from an important noble family

duel   a fight between two people, with swords or guns

examination   a test to find out what someone knows or can do

fire *(v)*   to shoot with a gun at somebody or something

fleet   a large group of ships

frigate   a fast warship

galley   a long ship, rowed by large numbers of people (often slaves)

God (My God, Good God)   expressions of surprise or fear

grapnel a piece of metal with hooks, for catching hold of an enemy ship

harbour a place close to land where ships can stop safely

hold *(n)* the place below the deck on a ship where cargo is carried

jolly boat a small ship's boat that holds seven seamen

lamp a kind of light which burns oil

lieutenant a ship's officer, above a midshipman and below a captain

longboat a ship's boat that holds forty seamen

load *(v)* to put things into something (e.g. cargo into a ship, bullets into a gun)

mast a tall piece of wood that stands on a ship to hold the sails

mathematics the study of numbers and shapes

midshipman a young ship's officer, below a lieutenant

miss-fire when a loaded gun fails to fire

oar a long piece of wood, with one flat end, for rowing a boat

parole a promise by a prisoner that he will not try to escape

pistol a small gun which can be held in the hand

point *(v)* to show with your finger where something is

position the place where someone or something is

privateer a ship used for attacking and robbing other ships

prize (in this story) a ship which has been taken prisoner by another ship

promotion getting a higher or more important job than the one you had before

rat a small grey animal with a long tail (bigger than a mouse)

revolution a complete, sudden, and often violent change in the government of a country

rope very thick, strong string

second (in a duel) *(n)*   a person who helps somebody fighting a
  duel
slave   a person who is owned by another person and who works
  without pay
steer   to turn a wheel to guide a ship, car, etc.
telescope   a long instrument with special glass that makes
  distant things look bigger and nearer
war   fighting between two or more countries
weak   not strong
whip *(n)*   a long piece of leather or rope for hitting people or
  animals
whist   a card game

Mr Midshipman Hornblower

ACTIVITIES

Before Reading

1 **Read the story introduction on the first page, and the back cover. What do you know now about the story? Answer these questions.**

On a 1790s sailing ship of war . . .

1 where did people sleep?
2 what did people eat?
3 what were the possible dangers?

In 1793 . . .

4 which country was Britain at war with?
5 who was the youngest officer on the ship, and how old was he?
6 what health problem did he have at first?

2 **Can you guess what will happen in the story? Circle Y (Yes) or N (No) for each of these ideas.**

1 Hornblower loses a ship with a valuable cargo. Y/N
2 He takes an enemy ship prisoner, and receives promotion. Y/N
3 He falls in love with a woman passenger. Y/N
4 He fights another duel, and this time he is injured. Y/N
5 He is taken prisoner by the French, but escapes. Y/N
6 His ship goes down, and he has to swim back to land. Y/N
7 He helps to save Spanish sailors from drowning. Y/N
8 In the end, he becomes an admiral. Y/N

While Reading

Read Chapter 1, down to the bottom of page 11. Who said this, and to whom? Who or what were they talking about?

1 'What will he do when we *really* go to sea?'
2 'Oh dear! Mathematics would be more useful to you.'
3 'It could happen to anyone.'
4 'It will pass the time.'
5 'You know too much about this game.'
6 'There is only one answer to that.'
7 'I'd rather die!'
8 'So you won't change your mind?'

Before you read to the end of the chapter, try to guess what happens. Circle Y (Yes) or N (No) for each of these ideas.

1 Hornblower is injured in the duel. Y/N
2 Simpson is too frightened to fire his pistol, although his is the loaded one. Y/N
3 Following the captain's orders, the seconds make sure that neither of the pistols is loaded. Y/N
4 Lieutenant Masters stops the duel after Hornblower has fired his pistol. Y/N
5 After the duel, Hornblower is famous on the ship for his bravery rather than his seasickness. Y/N
6 After the duel, Simpson apologizes to Hornblower, and they become friends. Y/N

Read Chapter 2, down to the bottom of page 30. Are these sentences true (T) or false (F)? Rewrite the false sentences with the correct information.

1 The *Marie Galante* was a Spanish warship.
2 Hornblower was ordered to sail the ship back to England.
3 The hold was dry because the rice was taking in the water.
4 They threw the rice out, and saved the ship.
5 Hornblower and his men took the privateer prisoner.
6 On the privateer, Hornblower slept in the captain's berth.

Before you read to the end of Chapter 2, can you guess the answers to some of these questions?

1 How will Hornblower escape from the French privateer?
2 Will the French book on mathematics for seamen be useful for Hornblower's escape plan? If so, how?
3 When Hornblower sees his captain again, will he be punished for losing the *Marie Galante*, and if so, how? Or will Hornblower punish himself in some way?

Read Chapter 3. Choose the best question-word for these questions, and then answer them.

Where / Who / Why

1 ... was the *Indefatigable* at the beginning of this chapter?
2 ... were tied to their seats until they died?
3 ... did the English in Gibraltar have to buy food from?
4 ... couldn't the *Indefatigable* attack the Spanish galleys?
5 ... was the Spanish galley pulling the jolly boat along?

6 . . . was the first to climb on to the Spanish galley?

7 . . . was Hornblower so surprised to win the fight?

8 . . . was the nearest of the *Indefatigable*'s boats when the galley's Spanish flag came down?

9 . . . did Captain Pellew offer Hornblower promotion?

Read Chapter 4, down to the bottom of page 64, and then answer these questions.

1 Which ship was Hornblower taking to England, and why?

2 What did Hornblower learn at the Admiral's dinner?

3 How did Hornblower find himself in the middle of an enemy fleet?

4 What happened to the despatches?

5 What two pieces of news did Hornblower receive after four months in the Spanish prison?

6 What did Hornblower get in return for his parole?

7 How did Hornblower save three survivors from the Spanish privateer on the rocks?

Before you read to the end of Chapter 4, what do you think is going to happen? Choose endings for these sentences.

1 Hornblower has a chance to escape on an English ship . . .
   a) and takes it.   b) but refuses to break his parole.

2 Hornblower stays in prison in Ferrol for . . .
   a) a few more months.   b) another three years.

3 Hornblower is given his freedom . . .
   a) when the war ends.   b) because he saved Spanish lives.

After Reading

1 Here is Hornblower's letter to Kitty Cobham when he was set free from the Spanish prison. Put the sentences in the right order, and join them with these linking words to make a paragraph of five sentences. Start with number 2.

and / although / because / but / but / who / whose / so

Dear Kitty Cobham,

1 _____ offered to take me back to Britain,

2 It did indeed give me great happiness two years ago to hear that you had handed over the despatches safely,

3 _____ I managed to save the lives of three Spaniards,

4 Three survivors were able to jump into the boat,

5 _____ ship broke up on the rocks off the Spanish coast.

6 All ten of us were picked up later by an English captain,

7 _____ the sea was very rough that day,

8 _____ now I write to tell you some good news of my own.

9 _____ we had to spend the night out at sea.

10 _____ of course I could not break my parole.

11 I was able, with the help of six Spanish fishermen, to take a small boat out to the ship.

12 _____ we could not get back to the harbour in the dark

13 I have just been given my freedom by the King of Spain

All best wishes for your health and happiness,

Horatio Hornblower

2 **Lieutenant Masters told Captain Keene about the duel that Hornblower and Simpson were going to fight (see page 11). Complete Keene's side of the conversation.**

MASTERS: I'm afraid that two of the midshipmen are planning to fight a duel, sir.

KEENE: _____

MASTERS: Simpson, and young Horatio Hornblower.

KEENE: _____

MASTERS: I understand Simpson accused Hornblower of cheating at whist, sir, and then refused to apologize.

KEENE: _____

MASTERS: Pistols, sir. They're having one pistol loaded and the other unloaded, to allow one man to survive.

KEENE: _____

MASTERS: But what if I *can't* persuade them, sir?

KEENE: _____

MASTERS: Yes, sir. Very good idea, sir. I'll do that.

3 **Put these words from the story into four groups under these headings. There are four words which don't quite fit into any group. Which are they?**

TYPES OF SHIP	PARTS OF A SHIP
TYPES OF WEAPONS	SHIP'S OFFICERS

admiral, cabin, cannon, captain, cargo, crew, cutlass, cutter, deck, duel, fleet, frigate, galley, hold, lieutenant, mast, midshipman, pistol, privateer, whip

4 Perhaps this is what some of the characters in the story were thinking. Which characters are they, and what has just happened in the story?

1 'Here comes the Spanish officer. I must hold my head high, and look very cold and proud. He'll probably kiss my hand. I just hope he doesn't notice that I look fatter on one side than on the other!'

2 'My God! Look at them running along the deck! That's a bad sign. We'll never be able to save the ship now. Poor Mr Hornblower! It's his first command, too.'

3 'Was I like that when I was his age, so sure of what's right and what's wrong? He really wanted to come back to England with me, but he wouldn't break his word. Well, a promise is a promise, I suppose.'

4 'If he thinks I'm going to apologize, he's wrong! He's the one who cheated! He'll never be man enough to go ahead with the duel anyway – he's just a stupid, seasick boy!'

5 'I suppose I'll be in a British prison for the rest of the war now. I just can't understand how the fire started. I'm sure it wasn't an accident. I think it was that English officer, Hornblower. But how did he do it?'

6 'Excellent work, I must say. Valuable prize, a Spanish galley. The danger didn't seem to worry him at all – going into battle with six men and a jolly boat! Well, well! Think I'll try him out as a lieutenant, in poor Soames's place.'

5 Here is Hornblower's report for Captain Pellew, explaining how he lost the *Marie Galante* (see page 35). Choose one suitable word for each gap.

Everything went well at _____. I made my seamen _____ me, and kept the _____ crew under control. I _____ the sails repaired, and _____ which direction we would _____ in. I checked the _____, with Matthews, to see _____ she was taking in _____, and although I was _____ to see it was _____, I thought no more _____ it. I did not _____ what was happening down _____ until the next day, _____ the French captain politely _____ me that we were _____ a large cargo of _____. Immediately we tried to _____ the hole in the _____ of the ship, but _____ had already got in. _____ the rice in the _____ got bigger and bigger, _____ appeared between the wooden _____ of the deck. We _____ out some of the _____ of rice, but the _____ was low in the _____, and I decided to _____ her. She went down _____ after that.

6 Here are some new chapter titles. Four of them do not fit any chapter. Find them, and say why they don't fit. Then match the other titles to the right chapters, and say which you prefer.

- Despatches for an Actress
- Hornblower's Fighting Fever
- A Game of Cards
- Freedom for the Slaves
- Losing the *Marie Galante*
- Hornblower's Mistake
- Escape on the *Syrtis*
- A Duel to the Death
- Heads or Tails?
- Rice Catches Fire
- Three Against Twelve
- Keeping a Promise

ABOUT THE AUTHOR

Cecil Scott Forester was born in Cairo to British parents, in 1899. He went to a London public school, and studied to be a doctor, before becoming a writer. His first successful novel, *Payment Deferred* (1926), set in World War I, was made into a play and later a film. This was followed by a book about the life of Nelson, and two well-known novels, *Death to the French* (1932) and *The Gun* (1933), about the British war against the French, which took place in Spain and Portugal in the early 1800s. For a time Forester was a script writer in Hollywood, then became a war reporter in the Spanish Civil War and World War II. During these years he continued to write novels, and one of these, *The African Queen* (1935), became famous as a film by John Huston in 1952, starring Katharine Hepburn and Humphrey Bogart (who won an Oscar for his acting).

After World War II Forester's health became poor, and he moved to California, in the USA. He died in 1966.

C. S. Forester's best-known novels are the very popular Hornblower books, which by the time of his death had sold eight million copies. Horatio Hornblower was partly based on the life of Admiral Horatio Nelson, Britain's most famous admiral, and a hero of the Napoleonic Wars in Europe from 1799 to 1815. A series of twelve novels, all full of accurate historical detail, follows Hornblower's career and adventures, from a seasick young officer in *Mr Midshipman Hornblower* to a famous admiral in *Hornblower in the West Indies*.

There has been a film and also a recent television series of some of the Hornblower stories.

ABOUT BOOKWORMS

OXFORD BOOKWORMS LIBRARY

Classics • True Stories • Fantasy & Horror • Human Interest
Crime & Mystery • Thriller & Adventure

The OXFORD BOOKWORMS LIBRARY offers a wide range of original and adapted stories, both classic and modern, which take learners from elementary to advanced level through six carefully graded language stages:

Stage 1 (400 headwords)	Stage 4 (1400 headwords)
Stage 2 (700 headwords)	Stage 5 (1800 headwords)
Stage 3 (1000 headwords)	Stage 6 (2500 headwords)

More than fifty titles are also available on cassette, and there are many titles at Stages 1 to 4 which are specially recommended for younger learners. In addition to the introductions and activities in each Bookworm, resource material includes photocopiable test worksheets and Teacher's Handbooks, which contain advice on running a class library and using cassettes, and the answers for the activities in the books.

Several other series are linked to the OXFORD BOOKWORMS LIBRARY. They range from highly illustrated readers for young learners, to playscripts, non-fiction readers, and unsimplified texts for advanced learners.

Oxford Bookworms Starters   *Oxford Bookworms Factfiles*
Oxford Bookworms Playscripts   *Oxford Bookworms Collection*

Details of these series and a full list of all titles in the OXFORD BOOKWORMS LIBRARY can be found in the *Oxford English* catalogues. A selection of titles from the OXFORD BOOKWORMS LIBRARY can be found on the next pages.

Lord Jim

JOSEPH CONRAD

Retold by Clare West

A hundred years ago a seaman's life was full of danger, but Jim, the first mate on board the *Patna*, is not afraid of danger. He is young, strong, confident of his bravery. He dreams of great adventures – and the chance to show the world what a hero he is.

But the sea is no place for dreamers. When the chance comes, on a calm moonlit night in the Indian Ocean, Jim fails the test, and his world falls to pieces around him. He disappears into the jungles of south-east Asia, searching for a way to prove himself, once and for all . . .

Desert, Mountain, Sea

SUE LEATHER

Three different parts of the world, but all of them dangerous, lonely places. Three different women, but all of them determined to go – and to come back alive!

Robyn Davidson walked nearly 3,000 kilometres across the Australian desert – with a dog and four camels.

Arlene Blum led a team of ten women to the top of Annapurna – one of the highest mountains in the world. Only eight came down again.

Naomi James sailed around the world alone, on a journey lasting more than 250 days.

Three real adventures – three really adventurous women.

Treasure Island

ROBERT LOUIS STEVENSON

Retold by John Escott

'Suddenly, there was a high voice screaming in the darkness: "Pieces of eight! Pieces of eight! Pieces of eight!" It was Long John Silver's parrot, Captain Flint! I turned to run . . .'

But young Jim Hawkins does not escape from the pirates this time. Will he and his friends find the treasure before the pirates do? Will they escape from the island, and sail back to England with a ship full of gold?

We Didn't Mean to Go to Sea

ARTHUR RANSOME

Retold by Ralph Mowat

The four Walker children never meant to go to sea. They had promised their mother they would stay safely in the harbour, and would be home on Friday in time for tea.

But there they are in someone else's boat, drifting out to sea in a thick fog. When the fog lifts, they can turn round and sail back to the harbour. But then comes the wind and the storm, driving them out even further across the cold North Sea . . .

The Eagle of the Ninth

ROSEMARY SUTCLIFF

Retold by John Escott

In the second century AD, when the Ninth Roman Legion marched into the mists of northern Britain, not one man came back. Four thousand men disappeared, and the Eagle, the symbol of the Legion's honour, was lost.

Years later there is a story that the Eagle has been seen again. So Marcus Aquila, whose father disappeared with the Ninth, travels north, to find the Eagle and bring it back, and to learn how his father died. But the tribes of the north are wild and dangerous, and they hate the Romans . . .

David Copperfield

CHARLES DICKENS

Retold by Clare West

'Please, Mr Murdstone! Don't beat me! I've tried to learn my lessons, really I have, sir!' sobs David.

Although David is only eight years old, Mr Murdstone does beat him, and David is so frightened that he bites his cruel stepfather's hand. For that, he is kept locked in his room for five days and nights, and nobody is allowed to speak to him.

As David grows up, he learns that life is full of trouble and misery and cruelty. But he also finds laughter and kindness, trust and friendship . . . and love.